Joan Copeland

Onwards and Upwards Publishers

Berkeley House, 11 Nightingale Crescent,
Leatherhead, Surrey, KT24 6PD.
www.onwardsandupwards.org

First edition published by Word for Life Trust (2003).

Second edition published by Onwards and Upwards
Publishers (2014).

Printed in the UK.

ISBN: 978-1-910197-07-3
Cover design: Leah-Maarit

CONTENTS

MORNING PRAYER

Every morning, Lord,
   you knock at the door of my life.
Most days I keep you
   standing on the doorstep,
   saying how busy I am.
This morning you ask courteously,
   'May I come in?'
I grudgingly allow you
   to step into the hall.
I am conscious
   of the grime of past sins,
   the muddle evident
   on the threshold of my life.
It's obvious you want to stay.
I let you into the front room,
   brush clutter from a chair
   to let you sit.
In the end, Lord, you offer
   to spring clean for me.
Thank you.

RUSH HOUR

Father, when I travel in the rush hour
    there are so many people.
Smelly, awkward people
    with umbrellas and briefcases
    that prod and bump against me.
I get annoyed.

But when I think
    you know them all by name,
    each one of them you see
    and know and love,
Father, I'm overwhelmed
    by the greatness of your love.

Help me to love them too.

FOG

I'm in the driving seat.
I peer ahead, trying to see.
Wipers sweep,
    demister clears the screen.
I peer and peer, straining my eyes.
The world is blank,
    a wet white wall
    encompassing the car.
Sometimes I think I recognise
    a tree, a gate.
Then I am lost again,
    exhausted by the strain.

My way through life
    is sometimes fogbound too.
I strain to see.
I don't know where I am,
    which way to go.
Burst through the fog,
    disperse it with your sunshine, Lord,
    show me the way ahead
    and I will go.

WASHING UP

Washing up, piles of it,
    after every meal.
Looking at that greasy mess,
    you know, Lord, how I feel.

I wonder if you feel the same
    when my sins I confess?

Like the dirty cups and dishes
I need washing every day.
Help me, Lord, as I wash dishes,
    and wash all my sins away.

POINTS OF PEACE

Points of peace in a busy day,
Moments when there's
    nothing I can do,
While the washing dries
    at the launderette,
Standing in the supermarket queue,
When the bus is late
    and my feet are cold,
Waiting for kettle to boil
    or meat to stew.

Then, Lord, I pause
    and know you're here,
Feel your presence and peace
    as I think of you.
I come with you to a quiet place,
    then raise my eyes,
    and the world is new.

GARDEN OF DELIGHTS

Each day an empty basket
  with which we enter
  the garden of your delights.

Sometimes it is you who gives to us
  a flower, a luscious fruit,
Sometimes the under-gardeners
  load us with vegetables,
And sometimes we pick ourselves
  your bounteous fare.

But sometimes, deliberately or not,
  our basket fills with weeds,
  with heavy stones
  and slugs and snails.

Then, at the end of day, let us unpack
   our basket of delights,
   get rid of weeds, enjoy each bloom,
   savour the luscious fruit,
   process the vegetables.
   and let them nourish us.
Give thanks for everything.

GARDENING

Creator God,
    you gave to man a garden
    to fill and cultivate
    and bring forth fruit.
You gave us all, Lord,
    longing to be gardeners,
    to grow green plants and flowers.

There were no weeds
    in Adam's garden though,
    while mine is full of them.
More time I spend
    removing all the weeds
    than planting seed.

Lord Jesus, Mary thought
    you were the gardener.
Weed from my life
    all that stops growing fruit for you.

GROWTH

Lord, I fret and rush,
    and try to organise my busy life.

But when I watch the bulbs in spring
    first poking through the earth,
    then growing up,
    then gradually
    buds opening in the sun,
I realise growth takes time
    not busy effort.

Lord, help me to be still
    to let your sunshine open up my life
    for fruitful growth.

THE POTTER

You are the Potter, Lord,
   and we the clay.

My life is like a shelf of little pots.
Many are ugly and misshapen things.
They need to be remade,
   rethrown by you,
   stamped with your Name.

But in the end
   you, Lord, must take them all,
   mould them together
   in one single lump,
   throw them upon your wheel,
   fire with your love,
   fill with your Spirit.
Then shall I be whole,
   a fitting vessel for your glory, Lord.

IN HIS HANDS

Hands cupped gently,
   he cradles me
   when I am hurt,
   as one holds gently
   a butterfly
   with lightest touch.

Firmly he grasps
   the tool he'll use,
   guiding its path,
   as one grasps firmly
   chisel or pen
   to do its task.

Tightening his grip,
   He squeezes me,
   I share his pain,
   as one grips tightly
   the sharing hand
   in agony.

Rest

Here, on a little grassy patch of land
   beneath the oak tree's shade,
   watching the mountain stream
   and listening to its unending song,
   let your ears rest
   in soothing constant sound,
   let body rest
   on yielding sunlit turf,
   so mind will rest,
   yes rest,
   in my own presence safe.

TERROR

Not the bomb now,
   a distant threat,
   but present terror, Lord,
   for me, today.

When I am on the bus or tube,
   will I arrive alive?
When passing neighbours
   in the street,
   are they a threat?
Am I safe anywhere?

Lord, teach me to trust in you,
   in whom I live,
   for my own life.
Teach me to trust in others,
   whom you love.
And teach us all to love
   before it is too late.

TIME

Only in the country pub
   can I spend half an hour
   discussing on what day,
   what time of day,
   to plant broad beans.

Our life is crammed
   with time-saving machines,
   yet only here,
   with folks who don't save time,
   do I have time.

Time to watch the seeds that grow,
   wait for the leaven in the dough,
   things that you likened
      to your Kingdom, Lord,
   the Kingdom that our modern world
      cannot afford.

Mobile Phone 1

I dial the number
    when I feel I need to reach you, Lord.

Sometimes it rings and rings
    – but no one answers.

Sometimes it is engaged
    – I'll try again.

Sometimes it's number unobtainable
    – a hostile shriek.

And at all times
    you stand beside me, Lord,
    saying, 'I am here.
    You do not need to dial.
The telephone is your invention:
    a ritualist device
    which you feel connects us.'

MOBILE PHONE 2

Your ring tones sound, dear Lord,
   around us all the time:
   the beauty of a sunset;
   cry of need;
   whisper of conscience;
   other people's eyes.

The ring tones sound,
   demanding a response,
   to press the button,
   ask, 'Who's there?'
   and listen to your voice.

And if I do not answer,
   it will go on ringing for a while
   and then will stop.
And I will never know
   what word you had for me.

PRAYER FOR A FRIEND

I pray
    for what I always pray for you:
    for peace, his deep down peace,
    a calm and deepest peace
    beneath the ruffled wavelets
    of your life,
    threshing the topmost layers
    into spume
    which frets and foams.

I pray that deep down peace
    might upwards spread its influence
    in your life,
    and all will be serene.

A CAT'S PRAYER

Lord, I would like to be a purring pet,
   the symbol of a cosy fireside peace.
But, Lord, one person I can't stand.
She strokes me up the wrong way
   every time.
My hackles rise, my tail begins to lash,
   my claws are sharp
   and itching to come out.

Lord, teach me why it is,
   and how she feels.
Perhaps when she was young,
   a cat like me
   clawed at her face and legs.
Maybe she has an allergy:
   I make her sneeze.
Or does she envy me,
   and wish she were a cat?

Lord, take me on your lap,
   smooth down the ruffled fur,
   velvet my claws
   and teach me how to purr.

SHUT YOUR MOUTH

I jump in and defend my faith.
I sock it to them, Lord.

I turn to you, Lord.
What was your defence?
They accused you wrongly.
   and twisted what you said.
Yet you said nothing.
You answered not a word.
You shut your mouth.
You knew that you had done
   all that your Father willed.
In him was your defence.
You held your peace
   and you were justified.
He raised you from the dead.

Next time, Lord,
   when I leap to your defence,
   let me remember you
   and shut my mouth.

THE SUFFERING CHRIST

And must you always stand alone,
   the Holy One?
Misunderstood, rejected
   by those to whom you came
   reacting to your searching light,
   your ever-living flame.

But if a grain of wheat remain,
   it must remain alone.
The increase of that wheat can come
   only when 'tis sown.

So by your death,
   my Christ, my God,
You draw us unto thee,
   that in your suffering
   we might share
   in your eternity.

THE GIFT

I struggle, Lord, to render it to you,
   that offering, such a little thing,
   yet so great in my eyes.
I wrench it from me,
   lay it grudgingly upon thine altar
       stone.

Look how it lies there, small,
   the tiniest token, hardly to be seen,
   of all the gifts that you have given
       me.

Yet you accept, joyfully,
   gladly and with gratitude,
   not just that gift, but its heart value,
All the cost to me
   you take unto yourself,
   endow it with such value
   as I thought it had.

So when I reach that place
   where I can see
   how paltry was the gift I offered thee,
   then will you give it back, all
      glorified,
  precious as if I died to give it thee.

BIRTHDAY

New born babe in Christ,
    ageless in him,
    begotten in his mind
    before created time.
Born for his praise
    throughout eternity.
Born from his love
    that you his love might be.

OFFERING

We in the prime of life
    offer you bread, fresh baked,
    on golden plate.
But when our heads grow grey,
    You hold the silver chalice
    with the wine,
    a lifetime now mature,
    the vintage of our years.

LEAVING HOME

My children leaving home,
   rejecting all I'd give.
Courageously, in innocence,
   choosing their way to live.

Jesus left Nazareth.
Did Mary feel like me
   as he carved out a brave new life,
   then died upon the tree?

Did Mary blame herself?
Or had she grace to see
   the gift that every child requires,
   the freedom to live free?

CHRISTMAS

And did the angels then return
　　to trembling sheep upon the hill
　　and comfort them, left all alone,
　　protecting from the wolves that kill?

We too leave those for whom we care
　　at Christmas time, to worship thee,
　　to kneel ourselves in stable bare
　　the Babe of Bethlehem to see.

Lord, send thine angels to our homes
　　to guard and comfort those we love,
　　that they who worship not with us
　　may peace, goodwill hear from
　　　　above.

"YOU DID IT UNTO ME"

"Inasmuch as you have done it
   to the least of these, you did it unto
      me."
So you said, Lord.
How often have we thought,
   as we some action for another took,
   we did it unto thee.
How that thought warmed our heart,
   as we felt sure
   that gratitude from you
   was quite enough for what we did.

But to receive on your behalf,
   dear Lord,
   is quite another thing.
You promised no reward for that.
That we should bear
   your gracious part,
   imitate your humble heart,
   helpless become,
   that others might serve you in us,
   for their reward.

FAILURE

A silver cross
   against the midnight blue
   of sorrows manifest,
   yet hidden from the world.

I look, Lord, at your cross
   and think of you.
You came and loved and gave.
You lived among the poor and
               prostitutes,
   the refuse and the dregs of
               humankind.
You healed them, loved and cared,
   with no support,
   and at the end you died
   alone.

Not a success.
Nor are we, Lord.
Teach us to be content
   to follow you.

FORGIVENESS

Lord Jesus, you show us that
   forgiveness is better than revenge,
   love is stronger than hate,
   self-sacrifice more desirable
   than self-preservation.

Lord, hold us in the victory
   of your forgiveness,
   won so hardly for us on the cross,
   that we,
   being forgiven sinners,
   may forgive
   and love all those who
   seek to hurt us.

Kyrie Eleison

Mighty God,
  holding all that is,

Encircling your creation
  with your love,

Rendering to none evil for evil,
  good to all.

Compassion, loving-kindness,
  steadfast love.

Yes, Lord, have mercy.